T0129951

BLESSED
ADVENTURE

BLESSED ADVENTURE

*The Beatitudes and the
Journey toward God*

Dean Duncan

iUniverse, Inc.
Bloomington

Blessed Adventure
The Beatitudes and the Journey toward God

iUniverse books may be ordered through booksellers or by contacting:

iUniverse
1663 Liberty Drive
Bloomington, IN 47403
www.iuniverse.com
1-800-Authors (1-800-288-4677)

ISBN: 978-1-4620-1240-4 (sc)
ISBN: 978-1-4620-1760-7 (ebk)

Library of Congress Control Number: 2011906063

Printed in the United States of America

iUniverse rev. date: 05/26/2011

Acknowledgments

Thanks go to several people for their help with this project. Douglas Marks, PhD, gave encouragement and advice and graciously allowed me to borrow some of his ideas. Doug is a former Christian college professor and is currently a Christian church minister. Marilyn Moczygemba, MEd, applied her red pencil to the manuscript and provided suggestions. Marilyn was an elementary school teacher who retired as a principal. Phillip J. Walton, BSL, the minister at the church I attend, made me think (a terrible thing to do to someone).

Posthumously I thank Clifford Sherry, PhD, retired biology professor, for encouraging me to keep going and for recommending my publisher.

Most of the Bible study and research was done using Quick Verse Bible software. For Bible citations I have used *The World English Bible* instead of a better-known translation because of copyright restrictions.

And thanks to my wife, Barbara, for her patience as I put thoughts to paper (or to a disk storage device), during which time I wouldn't let her talk to me.

Preface

There was no blinding flash of light or thunderous noise when I suddenly knew that the first sentences of Jesus's Sermon on the Mount and the way to salvation are connected.

It wasn't like that at all.

Having taught the primary through adult levels in church Bible school, I have been a student of the scriptures for many years. In that time, I have benefited from the teaching of great preachers and Bible college professors who influenced my thinking and increased my faith. Over the years, I have been privileged to receive lessons on the verses in the Bible that are called "the Beatitudes."

During several years of presenting lessons on these verses to my students, I began to notice how much these verses relate to the elements in the progress of a person's becoming a Christian. *Blessed Adventure* is the result of that realization and over forty years of Bible study. No blinding light. No clap of thunder.

This study is based on the Bible because I believe it is the word of God. Why do I believe this? Here are three reasons:

I believe the Bible is from God because of its honesty. Most biographies written by people emphasize the strengths of their subjects and play down their weaknesses. The Bible presents its heroes complete with their mistakes and sinful lapses. To mention a few, Abraham twice told half-lies about his wife, Moses took credit for producing water in the wilderness, David committed adultery and murder, and Peter denied Christ three times. God caused the Bible to be written, and because he is perfect, his word is honest and true.

The number of manuscripts of scripture far surpasses that of all other historic and ancient literature. Historical and archaeological evidence continue to confirm that the Bible is what it claims to be, God's word.

Highly intelligent, educated people I know, such as those mentioned in the acknowledgements, believe the Bible to be inspired by God and believe that it contains truth for living and obediently following him.

For serious Bible study, I recommend a translation instead of a paraphrase. Translators do their best to go to the earliest, most accurate documents to bring forth, word for word, idea for idea, an accurate representation of the original meaning. Paraphrasers reword for clarity and meaning and usually use modern language. Examples of Bible translations are the New International Version, the King James Version and the New American Standard Version. Examples of paraphrases are *the Living Bible* and *The Message*.

When you study the Bible, I hope you will ask the Lord to guide you to his truth for your life. He has promised to do so.

Introduction

The Interaction of the Message of Salvation and the Beatitudes

The amazing facts of the Gospel's message are that Jesus, God's only Son, came to live on Earth, died on a cross, was buried, and on the third day arose from death (1 Cor. 15:1–7). Amazing, but true!

The good news of the Gospel is that this was done for you, and individually you can be saved from your sins. You start by hearing the news and believing the facts (Acts 16:31). You continue by turning to God (Acts 2:38), confessing your belief in those facts (Rom. 10:10), and being baptized into Jesus's death, burial and resurrection (Acts 2:38, Rom. 6:3–7). Living a life of service to him then becomes your privilege and duty (Rom. 6:16–18, 2 Tim. 2:11).

The Beatitudes encapsulate the attitude and conduct of those who receive and will continue to receive God's favor and rewards. At first glance, you may think that the Beatitudes show the attitudes and conduct of several people. I believe that they show a progression of attitudes and conduct of one person on the journey through a Godly life.

As you study the Beatitudes, you may notice that they relate to the progression God gives us in order to become his children. Applying the Gospel to yourself gives you the way into his presence and therefore, his way into our life. Moving through the elements of becoming closer to God found in the Gospel and related verses, you continue through the progression of your spiritual development as found in the Beatitudes. The elements of the good news and the elements of the Beatitudes support each other and intertwine in a beautiful way to enrich understanding of each. My ideas about this are contained in the following chapters.

Study of Matt. 5:3–10 will expand your appreciation of each step in becoming a child of God through Jesus Christ, and experiencing the process of moving toward God will enlarge your understanding of the Beatitudes.

The word *Beatitudes* means "blessings"; hence, the generally accepted name of this passage that mentions nine blessings.

Jesus gave a very important talk called "The Sermon on the Mount." From that talk here are the Beatitudes:

Seeing the multitudes, he went up onto the mountain. When he had sat down, his disciples came to him. He opened his mouth and taught them, saying:

> Blessed are the poor in spirit, for theirs is the Kingdom of Heaven.
> Blessed are those who mourn, for they shall be comforted.
> Blessed are the gentle, for they shall inherit the earth.
> Blessed are those who hunger and thirst after righteousness, for they shall be filled.
> Blessed are the merciful, for they shall obtain mercy.
> Blessed are the pure in heart, for they shall see God.
> Blessed are the peacemakers, for they shall be called children of God.

> Blessed are those who have been persecuted
>   for righteousness' sake, for theirs is the
>   Kingdom of Heaven.
> Blessed are you when people reproach you,
>   persecute you, and say all kinds of evil
>   against you falsely, for my sake. Rejoice,
>   and be exceedingly glad, for great is your
>   reward in heaven. For that is how they
>   persecuted the prophets who were before
>   you. (Matt. 5:3–12)

The word *blessed* comes from a root word that means "large," "lengthy," "fortunate," or "happy." But to be blessed is more than to be happy. The word was used in Greek literature, in the Septuagint (the Greek translation of the Old Testament), and in the New Testament to describe the kind of happiness that comes from receiving divine favor. The word can be rendered as "happy," but today we might say, "Congratulations!" In the New Testament, *blessed* is usually passive; God is the one who is blessing or favoring or congratulating the person. The word also appears in Ps. 1:1–3 and Revelations 1:3.

Are the actions and attitudes listed in the Beatitudes unrealistic expectations for people of our time? Not at all. They are standards for all of God's people of all times. Through them good things can come to us and to the whole world. As humans, we may never reach the full accomplishment of the standards, but we need to grow continually toward them through the rest of our lives. One of the main principles learned from studying them along with the elements of salvation is that they are achieved only through Jesus, not solely through our own effort or merit.

You will notice that the word "Yaweh" is used in *The World English Bible* (WEB), whereas you are probably accustomed to seeing the word "LORD." Both "LORD" and "Yaweh" are used to stand for the name of God.

For your convenience, I have brought in the Bible references alluded to in the introduction (please, always consider the context of the verses quoted):

1 Cor. 15:1–7

Now I declare to you, brothers, the Good News which I preached to you, which also you received, in which you also stand, by which also you are saved, if you hold firmly the word which I preached to you—unless you believed in vain. For I delivered to you first of all that which I also received: that Christ died for our sins according to the Scriptures, that he was buried, that he was raised on the third day according to the Scriptures, and that he appeared to Cephas, then to the twelve. Then he appeared to over five hundred brothers at once, most of whom remain until now, but some have also fallen asleep. Then he appeared to James, then to all the apostles.

1 Pet. 1:17–21

If you call on him as Father, who without respect of persons judges according to each man's work, pass the time of your living as foreigners here in reverent fear: knowing that you were redeemed, not with corruptible things, with silver or gold, from the useless way of life handed down from your fathers, but with precious blood, as of a faultless and pure lamb, the blood of Christ; who was foreknown indeed before the foundation of the world, but was revealed at the end of times for your sake, who through him are believers in God, who raised him from the dead, and gave him glory; so that your faith and hope might be in God.

Acts 16:31
They said, "Believe in the Lord Jesus Christ, and you will be saved—you and your household."

Acts 2:38
Peter said to them, "Repent and be baptized, every one of you, in the name of Jesus Christ for the forgiveness of sins. And you will receive the gift of the Holy Spirit.

Rom. 10:10
For with the heart, one believes unto righteousness; and with the mouth confession is made unto salvation.

Rom. 6:3–7
What shall we say then? Shall we continue in sin, that grace may abound? May it never be! We who died to sin, how could we live in it any longer? Or don't you know that all we who were baptized into Christ Jesus were baptized into his death? We were buried therefore with him through baptism to death, that just like Christ was raised from the dead through the glory of the Father, so we also might walk in newness of life. For if we have become united with him in the likeness of his death, we will also be part of his resurrection; knowing this, that our old man was crucified with him, that the body of sin might be done away with, so that we would no longer be in bondage to sin. For he who has died has been freed from sin.

Rom. 6:16–18

Don't you know that to whom you present yourselves as servants to obedience, his servants you are whom you obey; whether of sin to death, or of obedience to righteousness? But thanks be to God, that, whereas you were bondservants of sin, you became obedient from the heart to that form of teaching whereunto you were delivered. Being made free from sin, you became bondservants of righteousness.

2 Tim. 2:11
This saying is faithful: for if we died with him, we will also live with him.

Ps. 1:1–3
Blessed is the man who doesn't walk in the counsel of the wicked nor stand in the way of sinners nor sit in the seat of mockers.
But his delight is in Yaweh's law.
On his law he meditates day and night.
He will be like a tree planted by the streams of water,
That brings forth its fruit in season, whose leaf also does not wither.
Whatever he does shall prosper.

Rev. 1:3
Blessed is he who reads and those who hear the words of the prophecy, and keep the things that are written in it, for the time is at hand.

Chapter One

Hearing and *"Blessed Are the Poor in Spirit, for Theirs Is the Kingdom of Heaven."*

Is being poor in spirit something to be rewarded? How can it result in your receiving the Kingdom of Heaven?

Hearing the facts of the Gospel and the good news that you can enter into the facts to become God's person (Rom. 6:3–4) leads to another question. What was the reason for Jesus's sacrifice?

All people are separated from God because of the sin in their lives (Rom. 3:23). When I apply this to myself, I realize I have a problem:

- I am a sinner.
- I am not connected to God.
- I want to be connected to him.
- God requires a blood sacrifice for sin.
- The sacrifice needs to be perfect.
- I do not have a fitting sacrifice,
- not even myself, since I'm not perfect.
- God has furnished the perfect sacrifice!

If we want to be presented to God as holy (Col. 1:21–23), God requires a perfect blood sacrifice for our sins (Exod. 12:5 and Heb. 9:22), but we have no sacrifice to bring. Nothing we have is good enough; nothing we have is perfect. The good things we have done in our lives are not good enough, and they do not come close to making up for the sins we have committed. Nothing we own—even ourselves—is good enough or pure enough to serve as a sacrifice for our sins. We need something outside of ourselves, a perfect, unblemished sacrifice. Where can one be found? We must rely on God's grace.

We have nothing except hope in him. God has provided. Jesus lived a perfect life, so he is the perfect sacrifice we need. God gave us his perfect son (2 Cor. 5:21 and Heb. 4:14–15), the Lamb of God, to be our savior (Col. 2:13–14). Therefore, he is the only possible perfect sacrifice for our sins.

Spiritually we are no longer proud and self-sufficient. We are "poor in spirit." We know we cannot be reconciled with God on our own. We comprehend our utter spiritual destitution and our total need for the sacrifice God made for us in his son's death. We must rely on God's grace.

This concept of my being poor in spirit has been a hard one for me to accept. I was brought up to be self-reliant, ready to take care of myself. To admit that I needed someone outside myself to become right with God was difficult. I needed God to send Jesus to die in my place. It has taken several years to accept the idea that anything I could offer God is just not pure enough to bring to him. You may grasp it more quickly than I did, and I hope you do; but either way, it is a very important concept to grasp in beginning your journey toward God.

The ultimate reward is promised in Matthew 25:34: "Then the King will tell those on his right hand, 'Come, blessed of my Father, inherit the Kingdom prepared for you from the foundation of the world.'"

The Beatitude teaches that the Kingdom of Heaven belongs to those who are poor in spirit. It is an immediate reward because embracing our poverty of spirit humbles us and is essential to our starting on the journey toward God.

Here are the Bible verses mentioned in Chapter One:

Rom. 6:3–4
Or don't you know that all we who were baptized into Christ Jesus were baptized into his death? We were buried therefore with him through baptism to death, that just like Christ was raised from the dead through the glory of the Father, so we also might walk in newness of life.

Rom. 3:23
For all have sinned and fall short of the glory of God.

Col. 1:21–23
You, being in past times alienated and enemies in your mind in your evil works, yet now he has reconciled in the body of his flesh through death, to present you holy and without blemish and blameless before him, if it is so that you continue in the faith, grounded and steadfast, and not moved away from the hope of the Good News which you heard, which is being proclaimed in all creation under heaven; of which I, Paul, was made a servant.

Exod. 12:5
Your lamb shall be without blemish, a male a year old. You shall take it from the sheep, or from the goats.

Heb. 9:22
According to the law, nearly everything is cleansed with blood, and apart from shedding of blood there is no remission.

2 Cor. 5:21
For him who knew no sin he made to be sin on our behalf; so that in him we might become the righteousness of God.

Heb. 4:14–15
Having then a great high priest, who has passed through the heavens, Jesus, the Son of God, let us hold tightly to our confession. For we don't have a high priest who can't be touched with the feeling of our infirmities, but one who has been in all points tempted like we are, yet without sin.

Col. 2:13–14
You were dead through your trespasses and the uncircumcision of your flesh. He made you alive together with him, having forgiven us all our trespasses, wiping out the handwriting in ordinances which was against us; and he has taken it out of the way, nailing it to the cross.

For meditation or, as we say in Texas,
"Just ponderin'":

Think about listening and hearing, looking and seeing. Often we listen without really hearing much. Sometimes we look, but we do not see.

Our ears listen and our eyes look, but it is our minds and hearts that hear and see. While reading chapter 1, did I simply listen and look, or did I really hear and see God's truth and what was said about it? Do I need to go back over the material and pause to think about its meaning for me at this time and in my life situation?

Am I starting to realize my poverty of spirit? Do I have the common idea that the good things I have done will outweigh the bad? God has spent a lot of time and effort in the Bible to teach us that he requires not good deeds, but faith to have our sins permanently removed.

As I read the introduction and chapter 1, did I realize that the Gospel applies to me?

Is the general direction of my life "pretty good"? Is that what God wants?

Do I have anything to offer God? If not, what can I do?

Chapter Two

Believing and *"Blessed Are Those Who Mourn, for They Shall Be Comforted"*

Why are we being congratulated for mourning? Mourning what?

Are we lamenting the dead? Jesus did not encourage mourning for the dead. As we find in Matt. 8:21–22:

Another of his disciples said to him, "Lord, allow me first to go and bury my father." But Jesus said to him, "Follow me, and leave the dead to bury their own dead."

Is it our personal sins that we are mourning? Is it our consciousness of the cost of our sin and the resulting grief of the Father? Is personal death being mourned? The sins of the world? These concerns are certainly often part of the mourning process.

Believing what has been heard and realizing that we have no personal, individual spiritual value opens us to mourning. The mourning is for the sinful state in which we find ourselves and our spiritual deadness. We can do nothing for ourselves; we are "poor in spirit," and we grieve.

Knowledge of the fact that Jesus died for us brings home the reality of what we did to Jesus on the cross, and we mourn before God (Rom. 5:8). Let me make that more personal: I realize that Jesus was the sacrifice for my own sins, and I mourn.

Sin brings death. Look for life! What can be done about it? Turn to Christ!

As a result of starting to turn toward life, the process is begun: we are on the way toward being comforted by God through Jesus, his son.

> The Spirit of the Lord Yahweh is on me; because Yahweh has anointed me to preach good news to the humble. He has sent me to bind up the brokenhearted, to proclaim liberty to the captives, and release to those who are bound; to proclaim the year of Yahweh's favor, and the day of vengeance of our God; to comfort all who mourn; to appoint to those who mourn in Zion, to give to them a garland for ashes, the oil of joy for mourning, the garment of praise for the spirit of heaviness; that they may be called trees of righteousness, the planting of Yahweh, that he may be glorified. (Isa. 61:1–3)

> For the Lamb who is in the midst of the throne shepherds them, and leads them to springs of waters of life. And God will wipe away every tear from their eyes." (Rev. 7:17)

Our hearts are beginning to accept how much Jesus has done in paying for our sins. We find we are marvelously comforted, knowing our sins can be completely removed by his work on the cross and that we have life because of his astounding resurrection. We can have someone walking beside us in this journey, the Holy Spirit, the comforter (counselor) promised in John 14:16–17. The promise of comfort does not mean that God will make us comfortable; it means he will stand by us, support us, encourage us, and console us. As we lean on Jesus, we are leaning toward repentance.

When one is comforted, he learns to comfort others, for how could one comfort unless one has first been comforted oneself? Having received the ultimate comfort of knowing God has given us a way to have our sins removed, we are able to comfort other people as they face the trials of ordinary life and offer them the transcendent comfort of knowing their sins can be forgiven.

I have been growing in my ability to accept my own poverty of spirit, and my ability to mourn the state of my spiritual poverty continues as I mature. The older I become, the more clear it is to me that I am spiritually "broke" on my own, and I still grieve over this, but I also rejoice in the comfort the Holy Spirit provides.

*These are the verses I quoted in Chapter Two
(the others are included in the chapter):*

Rom. 5:8
But God commends his own love toward us, in that while
we were yet sinners, Christ died for us.

John 14:16–17
I will pray to the Father, and he will give you another
Counselor that he may be with you forever,—the Spirit of
truth, whom the world can't receive; for it doesn't see him,
neither knows him. You know him, for he lives with you,
and will be in you.

Meditate on these questions from Chapter Two:

Have you ever had a time in your life when you let it soak in that you are spiritually "broke"?

Did you mourn over that awareness and the idea that your sin caused Jesus to have to die?

A Bible study suggestion: Read chapter 53 of the book of Isaiah. It was written some seven hundred years before Jesus was born, but it feels like the author witnessed the crucifixion.

When you see Jesus dead in the tomb, do you comprehend and appreciate that it should have been you?

Chapter Three

Repentance and *"Blessed Are the Gentle, for They Shall Inherit the Earth"*

Having heard the Gospel message and believed the facts, the believer mourns over his or her condition. Something must be done. There stirs a desire to turn to God. This is the beginning of repentance.

Repentance has been referred to as doing an "about face," but I would call it executing "to the rear, march." The human journey through life embodies movement, either away from God or toward him. The unsaved person has been marching away from God. He or she learns of the need for God, does a 180-degree turn, and marches toward him. The general drift of his or her life has been in alienation from God. Now he or she seeks an ever-closer walk with Him through Christ.

A result of this turning and walking in a new direction is a gentleness (*meekness* in many Bible translations) arising out of inner strength—strength from the decision to live God's way, to search the scriptures for the Lord's will, and to act upon what is found there. This is gentleness, not as the world defines it, but a willingness to be controlled by the Maker of everything.

The quality of gentleness in life is not fear of what the outside world can do to an individual, but controlled strength. There is humility in submission to God's will, and there is power in knowing and carrying out that will.

Gentleness is not weakness. Think of a fast, powerful wild horse. With training and under the control of an experienced rider, the horse is not slower or weaker as it acts in concert with its master's will. The gentle (meek) person of God is like this: gentle but strong.

This idea of God's expecting us to be meek is especially difficult for men to grasp. Men have been taught most of their lives to be strong and to look out for themselves. When I have discussed this concept with men, sometimes it seems that it doesn't soak in at all. If you are having a hard time with this, think about the strong horse that is not weakened at all by submitting to his master. With God's help, you can be gentle and still be strong.

I have often been sarcastic in my conversation, but when I took this Beatitude to heart, I became aware that sarcasm is definitely not being gentle. Old habits die hard, but I think I am much less unkind in my speech than I once was. I try every day to improve.

This Beatitude promises that the gentle (humble) shall inherit the earth (the land, Ps. 37:11). I believe that this inheritance shall not come by conquering other people or lands but by achieving ultimate spiritual victory during the final disclosure of the Kingdom. This faith, demonstrated during our lives by our gentleness is the victory that overcomes the world. Who overcomes the world? Those who believe that Jesus is the Son of God (1 John 5:4–5).

Abraham looked for a city whose maker and builder was God (Heb. 11:8–10). We look and hope for no less than a place made by God. We anticipate a new Heaven and a new Earth. A new city is coming out of Heaven where God will live with humankind and we will live with him (Rev. 21:1–4). Abraham was promised a land. As Abraham's offspring by faith (Gal. 3:29), we, the gentle, will inherit a Kingdom!

Here are the verses used in Chapter Three:

Ps. 37:11
But the humble shall inherit the land, and shall delight themselves in the abundance of peace.

1 John 5:4–5
For whatever is born of God overcomes the world. This is the victory that has overcome the world: your faith. Who is he who overcomes the world, but he who believes that Jesus is the Son of God?

Heb. 11:8–10
By faith, Abraham, when he was called, obeyed to go out to the place which he was to receive for an inheritance. He went out, not knowing where he went. By faith, he lived as an alien in the land of promise, as in a land not his own, dwelling in tents, with Isaac and Jacob, the heirs with him of the same promise. For he looked for the city which has the foundations, whose builder and maker is God.

Rev. 21:1–4
I saw a new heaven and a new earth: for the first heaven and the first earth have passed away, and the sea is no more. I saw the holy city, New Jerusalem, coming down out of heaven from God, prepared like a bride adorned for her husband. I heard a loud voice out of heaven saying, "Behold, God's dwelling is with people, and he will dwell with them, and they will be his people, and God himself will be with them as their God. He will wipe away from them every tear from their eyes. Death will be no more; neither will there be

mourning, nor crying, nor pain, any more. The first things have passed away."

Gal. 3:29
If you are Christ's, then you are Abraham's seed and heirs according to promise.

Some thinking about Chapter Three:

Was that a new thought—that thing about looking for a city made by God? Do you ever think about it? What is it like? What kind of streets does it have? Does it have streetlights? Hint: it may take a little Bible study to find the answers.

Do you dream about being in the new city and the new earth?

Are you headed toward that city or away from it? Do you need to make that 180-degree turn in the direction of your life?

Do you have the strength to be gentle?

Chapter Four

Confession and *"Blessed Are Those Who Hunger and Thirst after Righteousness, for They Shall be Filled"*

As the repentant believer makes his way closer to God, he or she finds in the Bible that he or she should confess, letting other people know of his or her belief that Jesus is the Christ, the Son of the Living God. (Rom. 10:8–10).

The name "Jesus" shows he is wholly human. The word *Christ* means "the anointed one" or "the Messiah." The title "Christ" denotes that he is the King who was promised to his people. Jesus is the savior who was promised by God centuries before he was born. He is the only begotten Son of God, miraculously born of the Virgin Mary. The relationship of Son indicates he is wholly divine. He is truly God on Earth.

The believer's confession of faith declares that Jesus is to be his or her king and savior. The believer hungers and thirsts for righteousness, and maturing in this endeavor teaches him or her to define righteousness as "acting like

God acts." The believer resolves to do the right thing always.

Another important part of the confession is that everyone will eventually confess that Jesus is Lord and Messiah. You have the free choice now to confess, but others will confess at the end time when they realize how glorious God is in saving sinners through Jesus. Check verses 10 and 11 of the second chapter in the book of Philippians.

One of the most thrilling events I experience is witnessing a person coming to the front of a church gathering to be baptized or to join us, and hearing it stated publicly that he or she believes that Jesus is the Christ, the Son of the living God. It never fails to bring a tear to my eye.

The confession shows a desire for rightness with God that only Jesus can provide. There is a hunger to be seen as innocent in the eyes of God. There is thirst for his mercy and grace. His promise is that those who hunger and thirst for righteousness will be filled and that their spiritual need will be completely satisfied. In the journey of moving closer to God, confession before other believers demonstrates that one is well on the way.

Verses referred to in Chapter Four:

Rom. 10:8–10
"The word is near you, in your mouth, and in your heart"; that is, the word of faith, which we preach: that if you will confess with your mouth that Jesus is Lord, and believe in your heart that God raised him from the dead, you will be saved. For with the heart, one believes unto righteousness; and with the mouth confession is made unto salvation.

Phil. 2:10–11
Therefore God also highly exalted him, and gave to him the name which is above every name; that at the name of Jesus every knee should bow, of those in heaven, those on Earth, and those under the earth, and that every tongue should confess that Jesus Christ is Lord, to the glory of God the Father.

Think about this from Chapter Four:

Have you ever stood before people and told them, "I believe Jesus is the Christ, the Son of the Living God"?

If not, should you see to it that this happens?

Why is doing so now important in the overall scheme of things?

Are you having trouble coming to a decision about Jesus? Here is another suggested Bible study: read the book of John and then the book of Acts.

Chapter Five

Baptism and *"Blessed Are the Merciful, for They Shall Obtain Mercy"*

How can I know how pleasant it is for someone to receive a gift from me unless I have first received one? I did not know how to comfort someone who had just lost a loved one until I was comforted by others after the death of my brother. As a teacher, I could not have possibly known the thrill my students get upon learning a new concept unless I had felt that thrill myself.

I also cannot truly know what mercy is until I have received mercy. How can I show mercy to others unless I have received it myself?

Consider an example: Have you ever been stopped by a police officer for speeding? How thankful were you when the officer mercifully gave you just a warning ticket? You now have an inkling of how wonderful it can be to give mercy.

Entering into Christ's death, burial, and resurrection through baptism brings his mercy (Titus 3:4–5). Sins are forgiven. I deserved death for my sins, but I received life.

I was dead in my transgressions, but by grace I have been saved (Eph. 2:4–5). What mercy! Now I can communicate his mercy to other people. Now I can be more merciful to those I believe have wronged me.

When I wake up each morning, I try to remember to resolve for that day to be merciful. It does not always have to be a huge, dramatic display of mercy; it can be my saying "That's okay," when someone bumps into me at the grocery store. It can be as simple as holding the door for someone entering a building or letting another car enter my crowded lane from a side street. Mercy can manifest itself in showing patience when the normal human response might be to blow my top.

As a person trying to live the godly life, I need mercy from God and need to show mercy to others. I am to be forgiving because Christ forgave me (Col. 3:13, Eph. 4:32), yet the Beatitude promises mercy to the merciful. My motive for being merciful is my having received God's mercy for my sins, and the result of my being merciful to other people is my receiving mercy.

Showing mercy indicates power. God Almighty, the all-powerful one, showed me mercy. When I show mercy to someone, it confirms power, not weakness. Do you remember what I said about gentleness being power under control? Mercifulness reveals that controlled power.

Having received mercy at the time of my baptism, I am now at peace with God, other people, and myself (Rom. 5:1, Col. 3:15). Because I realize I have peace with God, I can grow in the realization of peace with myself. I no longer have to prove myself in the world; I am accepted by God as a member of his family. What more is there to prove?

This growth causes me to understand that peace with God, man, and self all go together.

Mercy is an attitude as well as an action. One who has received the mercy of God should learn to see other folks from God's perspective and should be moving through life with a mind-set of being ready at all times to dispense mercy. In my turning to God in repentance, God returns me to the world as a more merciful person.

Having been baptized, I have received the Holy Spirit (Acts 2:38), so I am beginning to see God's truth in the Bible more clearly and to apply it to myself (John 14:25–26). God's promise to satisfy my hunger and thirst for righteousness is being fulfilled.

Bible references in Chapter Five:

Titus 3:4–5
But when the kindness of God our Savior and his love toward mankind appeared, not by works of righteousness, which we did ourselves, but according to his mercy, he saved us, through the washing of regeneration and renewing by the Holy Spirit . . .

Eph. 2:4–5
But God, being rich in mercy, for his great love with which he loved us, even when we were dead through our trespasses, made us alive together with Christ (by grace you have been saved).

Col. 3:13
. . . bearing with one another, and forgiving each other, if any man has a complaint against any; even as Christ forgave you, so you also do.

Eph. 4:32
And be kind to one another, tenderhearted, forgiving each other, just as God also in Christ forgave you.

Rom. 5:1
Being therefore justified by faith, we have peace with God through our Lord Jesus Christ . . .

Col. 3:15
And let the peace of God rule in your hearts, to which also you were called in one body; and be thankful.

Acts 2:38
Peter replied, "Repent and be baptized, every one of you, in the name of Jesus Christ for the forgiveness of sins. And you will receive the gift of the Holy Spirit."

John 14:25–26
I have said these things to you, while still living with you. But the Counselor, the Holy Spirit, whom the Father will send in my name, he will teach you all things, and will remind you of all that I said to you.

Baptism

Some teach that baptism consists of sprinkling or pouring water on the person to be baptized. Others say that baptism in water is not necessary for a person to be considered saved.

First, let's look at the meaning of the word. *Baptism* is a transliteration of the Greek word *baptismos*. Transliteration means that the Greek letters were changed into English letters by the translators of the scriptures.

Greek scholars give several meanings to *baptismos*, including to dip, to immerse, and to plunge. The picture conveyed by the word is like that of a dish being dipped in water during the washing and rinsing process.

Some examples from the Bible should help in understanding what the Bible means by the word. As soon as Jesus was baptized, he went up out of the water (Matt. 3:16–17), so he must have been in the water in order to come up out of it. John baptized at a place where there was plenty of water (John 3:23). Phillip and the eunuch went down into the water in order for Phillip to baptize him (Acts 8:37–38). These verses indicate that baptism entails going into and under water and coming out again.

When is baptism needed? Again, let's look to the scriptures. When Peter preached the first Gospel sermon on the day of Pentecost, proclaiming Jesus, whom they had killed, to be Lord and Christ, the people who heard believed him and were cut to the heart. They asked, "What shall we do?" (Acts 2:36–37). This is the most important question anyone anywhere can ask. Upon the answer to this question and the acceptance of that answer rest the eternal destiny of every person now living.

Peter said to them, "Repent and be baptized, every one of you, in the name of Jesus Christ for the forgiveness of sins. And you will receive the gift of the Holy Spirit. For the promise is to you and to your children and to all who are far off, even as many as the Lord our God will call to himself" (Acts 2:38–39). This answer makes it very clear that repentant believers were to be baptized.

Others who accepted his message were baptized (Acts 2:41): the people in Samaria (Acts 8:12), the Ethiopian eunuch (Acts 8:38), gentiles in the house of Cornelius (Acts 10:48), Lydia (Acts 16:15), the Philippian jailor (Acts 16:30–33), people at Corinth (Acts 18:8), and the apostle Paul (Acts 22:16).

To those who teach that baptism is not necessary for a sinner to be saved, I pose some questions. How do you explain how we enter into Christ's death in order to be raised as he was raised to live a new life? (Rom. 6:3–4) How do you show people how to clothe themselves with Christ? (Gal. 3:27) How do you explain how to receive the circumcision of Christ? How do you explain how to be raised with him through faith? How do you explain how we are made alive in Christ? How do you explain exactly when all our sins were forgiven? (Col. 2:9–13) Without telling repentant sinners of their need to be baptized in water, how can you teach that they are saved? I suggest that the answer to each of these questions is that you cannot, as the scriptures plainly show.

As you can see, baptism is the next step in obedience for those who believe, repent, and confess. In Matt. 28:19–20, Jesus said, "Go and make disciples of all nations, baptizing them in the name of the Father and of the Son and of the Holy Spirit, teaching them to observe all things that I commanded you. Behold, I am with you always, even to the end of the age." Amen.

That was quite a few Bible verses. Here they are:

Matt. 3:16–17
Jesus, when he was baptized, went up directly from the water: and behold, the heavens were opened to him. He saw the Spirit of God descending as a dove, and coming on him. Behold, a voice out of the heavens said, "This is my beloved Son, with whom I am well pleased."

John 3:23
John also was baptizing in Enon near Salim, because there was much water there. They came, and were baptized.

Acts 2:36–37
"Let all the house of Israel therefore know certainly that God has made him both Lord and Christ, this Jesus whom you crucified." Now when they heard this, they were cut to the heart, and said to Peter and the rest of the apostles, "Brothers, what shall we do?"

Acts 2:41
Then those who gladly received his word were baptized. There were added that day about three thousand souls.

Acts 8:12
But when they believed Philip preaching good news concerning the Kingdom of God and the name of Jesus Christ, they were baptized, both men and women.

Acts 8:37–38
He commanded the chariot to stand still, and they both went down into the water, both Philip and the eunuch, and he baptized him.

Acts 10:48
He commanded them to be baptized in the name of Jesus Christ. Then they asked him to stay some days.

Acts 16:15
When she and her household were baptized, she begged us, saying, "If you have judged me to be faithful to the Lord, come into my house, and stay." So she persuaded us.

Acts 16:29–34
He called for lights and sprang in, and, fell down trembling before Paul and Silas, and brought them out and said, "Sirs, what must I do to be saved?" They said, "Believe in the Lord Jesus Christ, and you will be saved, you and your household." They spoke the word of the Lord to him, and to all who were in his house. He took them the same hour of the night, and washed their stripes, and was immediately baptized, he and all his household. He brought them up into his house, and set food before them, and rejoiced greatly, with all his household, having believed in God.

Acts 18:8
Crispus, the synagogue ruler, and his entire household believed in the Lord; and many of the Corinthians who heard him believed and were baptized.

Acts 22:16
Now why do you wait? Arise, be baptized, and wash away your sins, calling on the name of the Lord.

Rom. 6:3–4
Or don't you know that all we who were baptized into Christ Jesus were baptized into his death? We were buried therefore with him through baptism to death, that just like Christ was raised from the dead through the glory of the Father, so we also might walk in newness of life.

Gal. 3:27
For as many of you as were baptized into Christ have put on Christ.

Col. 2:9–13
For in him all the fullness of the Godhead dwells bodily, and in him you are made full, who is the head of all principality and power; in whom you were also circumcised with a circumcision not made with hands, in the putting off of the body of the sins of the flesh, in the circumcision of Christ; having been buried with him in baptism, in which you were also raised with him through faith in the working of God, who raised him from the dead.

Here are some questions to ponder
about Chapter Five:

Is sprinkling okay for baptizing in this day and time? Do you need to reread the previous section concerning the mode of baptizing?

Can you remember your baptism? If not, was it meaningful to you? Do you need to consider having yourself baptized as an adult? Wasn't Jesus around thirty years old when he was baptized by John?

In the paragraph above that is addressed to "those who teach," can you answer each of those questions as they apply to you?

Does showing mercy make you feel weak? Do you need to adjust your mind-set to accept the concept of "mercy through strength"?

Are you a merciful person? Do you need to take an attitude of mercy as you move through life? Are you spiritually strong enough to show mercy to people around you?

Chapter Six

Living the New Life and *"Blessed Are the Pure in Heart, for They Shall See God"*

Living a life for Christ is the only way to live after receiving his mercy. The believer becomes a servant to him (Rom. 6:22).

Having been cleansed of our sins (Heb. 10:14), we are now pure in heart (Acts 15:9)—not because of anything we have done, but by and through Jesus. His death was for us. God furnished the sacrifice required for our sins, and we have entered into Jesus's death through baptism (Rom. 6:3–4). When God the Father looks upon us, He sees Jesus (Gal. 3:27).

Only a purified heart is qualified to have God's law written on it. The law of Moses was written in stone, but the law of grace is written on our hearts (Heb. 8:10). Part of what this means is that we continue as his servants, not because we are required to do so, but because we want to do so.

It may seem arrogant to think of ourselves as "pure," but it is not. I once saw a bumper sticker that proclaimed that the driver was "Not perfect, but perfected." At first glance, that seemed arrogant, but upon deeper reflection, I saw it as a very humble statement. We are not perfect; we are perfected in God's sight through faith in Jesus and obedience to him.

Faith must be accompanied with action (James 2:14–17). Our purpose now is to live and teach so that others may know Jesus as we do. We are not perfect, as we are still human, but our hearts are pure, and we can teach with clear consciences (Heb. 9:14). Our actions reflect our pure hearts and pure motives. We have a single agenda, and it all relates to Jesus and seeking his Kingdom.

How can you seek the Kingdom? You should study the Bible on a regular basis, privately and in Bible classes. You should associate yourself with a church who bases her services and her service on the Bible. You should serve the community around you individually or as part of a group. You could even teach a Bible class at church or in your home.

You also teach through those of your actions that show mercy toward, patience with, and kindness to the people around you. For example, you might visit folks who are in hospitals or nursing homes. A man in our church takes communion and a short Bible lesson to residents at a local nursing home every Sunday morning.

Our human frailty will sometimes cause impure thoughts and actions to creep into our lives, impeding our journey. When we sin, we should confess those sins, and he will cleanse us (1 John 1:9), but the overall direction of our lives should demonstrate purity of heart.

Moses came as close as any living human to seeing God, speaking to him "face-to-face," yet Moses wanted to know (see) God (Exod. 33:13). This Beatitude tells us we will see

God. What more could we desire than to see him and know him?

While we are still on our journey here on Earth, we can see God in several areas:

> We can see him in the scriptures.
> We can see him in other people.
> We can see him in creation.
> We can see him in lives changed by Jesus.
> We are privileged to see him as Father.

People should be able to see God in the actions and reactions of our lives.

Only the pure in heart will see God in the ultimate sense. Purity is given to us by God because of our obedience to him, and our lives reflect that purity. We will be with him in glory, and we will see God (Col. 3:4)! Think of that: we will see him!

Chapter Six Bible quotes:

Rom. 6:22
But now, being made free from sin, and having become servants of God, you have your fruit of sanctification, and the result of eternal life.

Heb. 10:14
For by one offering he has perfected forever those who are being sanctified.

Acts 15:9
He made no distinction between us and them, cleansing their hearts by faith.

Rom. 6:3–4
Or don't you know that all we who were baptized into Christ Jesus were baptized into his death? We were buried therefore with him through baptism to death, that just like Christ was raised from the dead through the glory of the Father, so we also might walk in newness of life.

Gal. 3:27
For as many of you as were baptized into Christ have put on Christ.

Heb. 8:10
"For this is the covenant that I will make with the house of Israel.

After those days," says the Lord;
"I will put my laws into their mind,

I will also write them on their heart.
I will be their God, and they will be my people."

James 2:14–17
What good is it, my brothers, if a man says he has faith, but has no works? Can faith save him? And if a brother or sister is naked and in lack of daily food, and one of you tells them, "Go in peace, be warmed and filled;" and yet you didn't give them the things the body needs, what good is it? Even so faith, if it has no works, is dead in itself.

Heb. 9:14
How much more will the blood of Christ, who through the eternal Spirit offered himself without blemish to God, cleanse your conscience from dead works to serve the living God?

1 John 1:9
If we confess our sins, he is faithful and righteous to forgive us the sins, and to cleanse us from all unrighteousness.

Exod. 33:13
Now therefore, if I have found favor in your sight, please show me now your ways, that I may know you, so that I may find favor in your sight: and consider that this nation is your people."

Col. 3:4
When Christ, our life, is revealed, then you will also be revealed with him in glory.

Some meditation ideas from Chapter Six:

As a person of God, do I act like one? Is it possible to live as if I belong to God? Can I do it with the help of the Holy Spirit living in me? If my will is allowed to choose my route in life, how do I let the Spirit guide me instead?

Do I try to do good things to gain God's favor, or do I do good things because I have been brought into his family?

Chapter Seven

Continuing the Life, Showing Others the Way and *"Blessed Are the Peacemakers, for They Shall Be Called Children of God"*

The main reason for our existence as Christians is to tell other sinners the good news about Jesus—that he lived, died, was buried, and rose again and that there is a way to enter life with him. We do this by living Christ-like lives and by telling people how to obtain his peace through faith in him, repentance, and baptism.

Having received mercy, we have peace in our hearts and lives, and there is a balance of body, soul, and spirit before God, a wholeness in his sight. We need to spread peace. We take peace with us wherever we go. We desire to see other people whole, and we are healers through Jesus. Having peace with God from God makes us eligible to continue the spread of peace by teaching about Jesus and what he did for us in his death, burial, and resurrection (Matt. 28:18–20), leading folks to peace in him (Rom. 5:1, Phil. 4:7, Col. 1:19–20, James 3:17–18).

The Gospel moves us to be founders and promoters of peace. The Beatitude calls us Peace*makers*, not merely peace*keepers*. We should try to bring people into peace with God through the Gospel, and thereby into peace with themselves and with each other. We spread peace by teaching about Jesus and the only true peace that there is: the peace that he gives!

In doing one activity, you can always be certain you are doing the right thing. That activity is guiding people in study of the Bible.

One tip to help keep you from getting into arguments in your Bible study is to stay with the Bible as you teach, and avoid giving your own opinion. The people with whom you are dealing may be hearing God's truth for the first time, and they may have some incorrect ideas about God and ask questions. If they do, always go to the Scriptures for the answers. When we were studying the Bible in our home with the Christian Church preacher who eventually baptized my wife and me, one of the men of the church called on us. I asked him if he believed there really is a Heaven and a Hell, and he gave me a perfect answer. He said, "If the Bible says there is a Heaven and a Hell, I believe it." There was no argument, no discussion. If I had asked for proof from the Scriptures, I am sure he would have been able to show me.

Some of the most satisfying events in my life have occurred when I baptized people on whom I had called in their homes to show them the plan of salvation. A couple in our church gave their son my name as his middle name. What an honor! It was an even greater honor when I was asked to baptize him when he came to Christ!

This is a marvelous peace-distribution plan! Having heard of the plan from someone else, we become distributors of peace in Jesus. Distributors of peace! This is the best multi-level marketing system ever devised. The cost to become a distributor is both entirely free of any monetary charge and demanding of all we have, including our lives. The rewards are great, the return on investment even better, and the retirement plan beyond our wildest imaginations!

Note that we are called "children" of God—in the plural, not the singular. There are no Lone Rangers in the community of believers; this is a group effort. We bring healing and peace to the community, and the community brings healing and peace to us.

When we look at the Beatitudes this way, we can see how they affect both the saved and the unsaved. The saved are called to higher performance of their duties, and the unsaved are called to life in Jesus.

What greater reward for our peacemaking effort could we wish for than to be called children of God, as the Beatitude promises, and at the end of our time here to be greeted with, "Welcome, my son" or, "Welcome, my daughter"?

Chapter Seven verses:

Matt. 28:18–20
Jesus came to them and spoke to them, saying, "All authority has been given to me in heaven and on earth. Go, and make disciples of all nations, baptizing them in the name of the Father and of the Son and of the Holy Spirit, teaching them to observe all things that I commanded you. Behold, I am with you always, even to the end of the age." Amen.

Rom. 5:1
Being therefore justified by faith, we have peace with God through our Lord Jesus Christ . . .

Phil. 4:7
And the peace of God, which surpasses all understanding, will guard your hearts and your thoughts in Christ Jesus.

Col. 1:19–20
For all the fullness was pleased to dwell in him; and through him to reconcile all things to himself, by him, whether things on the earth, or things in the heavens, having made peace through the blood of his cross.

James 3:17–18
But the wisdom that is from above is first pure, then peaceful, gentle, reasonable, full of mercy and good fruits, without partiality, and without hypocrisy. Now the fruit of righteousness is sown in peace by those who make peace.

Some points to think about relating to Chapter Seven:

Am I a person of peace, one who brings chaos into a situation, or somewhere in between? As a peacemaker, do I project peace so those around me might want to have what I have?

Whom could I speak to about how they may have the peace of God?

Chapter Eight

Continuing in the Godly Life and *"Blessed Are Those Who Have Been Persecuted for Righteousness's Sake, for Theirs Is the Kingdom of Heaven"*

When a person lives for Jesus and spreads the good news about the peace of God and how to receive it, he or she may be mistreated by others for acting like Jesus. He or she may be tortured and punished or even killed, but he or she knows the Kingdom of Heaven belongs to him or her.

One note about persecution: Do not confuse suffering because of righteousness with persecution for other reasons. All humans suffer in varying degrees, and many are persecuted. The persecution referred to in this verse comes from doing God's will. As it is used in the Beatitude, "persecution" means to be pursued without giving up—faithful to the end.

I live in a nation where there is very little physical persecution of practicing Christians, but it is quite real in many parts of the world. Do not be surprised if it befalls you. Jesus was persecuted as he did God's will. Do you expect that you will not be persecuted as well (John 15:18)?

As a result of being persecuted, we have already received the Kingdom of Heaven. It is a "done deal." This gift of the Kingdom of Heaven is the same one that is received by the poor in spirit. Does this indicate a circular or continuous movement of the Beatitudes and the Gospel? I believe so.

As we go through the progression of becoming poor in spirit, mourning, gentleness, hungering, being merciful, becoming pure in heart, and peacemaking, the natural next step is to start the process over by telling another person about it. When that person goes through the cycle of hearing, believing, repenting, confessing, being baptized, and spreading the good news, the cycle starts again with his or her teaching someone new. As a result, as we teach about Jesus, we are strengthened in our own faith, and blessings multiply. May the cycle continue!

The verse for Chapter Eight:

John 15:18
If the world hates you, you know that it has hated me before
it hated you.

Some questions regarding chapter 8:

As my gratitude for being an adopted child of God becomes apparent in my actions and attitudes, am I ready to face some persecution?

Considering that Jesus suffered to the maximum, am I surprised that I may suffer physically, mentally, or psychologically?

Chapter Nine

Visual Presentations

Table 1. The Beatitudes

Condition	Scripture
Poor in Spirit	Matthew 5:3
Mourning	Matthew 5:4
Gentleness	Matthew 5:5
Hungering and Thirsting	Matthew 5:6
Mercy	Matthew 5:7
Purity of Heart	Matthew 5:8
Peacemaking	Matthew 5:9
Persecution	Matthew 5:10

Notice that coming to a realization about our own bankruptcy of spirit leads to mourning for our pitiful condition; the recognition that we can do nothing about it on our own and our decision to follow Jesus causes meekness. Then we begin to hunger and thirst for righteousness outside of ourselves, so we seek mercy at the cross of Jesus. This brings a purity of heart that we could never before achieve on our own. We want to be peacemakers, helping others come to peaceful righteousness, but being peacemakers can bring persecution upon us.

Then it starts over with telling new people and the new people telling others.

Table 2. Actions or Attitudes and Results

Condition	Reward
If I am:	*I will:*
poor in spirit	have the Kingdom of heaven
mourning	be comforted
gentle	inherit the Earth
hungering and thirsting	be fulfilled
merciful	receive mercy
pure of heart	see God
a peacemaker	be called a son/daughter of God
persecuted	have the Kingdom of Heaven

The cycle begins with the insight that we are poor in spirit and leads to our telling others about Jesus and, therefore, being persecuted. Then the cycle is already beginning again as the new hearer comes to see that he or she is poor in spirit. We also become stronger in our faith as we discuss these things with the people with whom we come in contact.

Table 3. Progression to Salvation

Stages	Scripture
Hearing	Rom. 10:17
Believing	Acts 16:29–31
Repenting	Acts 2:38
Confessing	Rom. 10:9–10
Being baptized	Acts 2:38; Rom. 6:3–5
Living for Jesus	James 2:14–17

Living for Jesus includes telling other people about him (Matt. 28:18–20). The process begins again with that person hearing the Gospel message.

Table 4. Blessings

My Actions and Attitudes	My Responses to God's Calling	The Work of God
	Hearing	
	Awareness of my condition	
Poor in Spirit	Realization that I can do nothing about it	Kingdom of Heaven
	Believing	
Mourning	Sadness because of my sin	Comfort
	Repenting	
Gentleness	Gentleness arising out of inner strength because of the decision to follow God's way	Inheritance of the Earth
	Confessing	
Hungering and Thirsting	Deep need for rightness with God outside of myself	Satisfaction
	Baptism	
Mercy	Showing and teaching God's mercy	Mercy
	Continuing in the New Life	
Purity of Heart	A purity (righteousness) only from God; inner peace	See God
	Showing Others	
Peacemaking	Spreading God's peace	Called sons/daughters of God
Persecution	Maltreatment by the world	Kingdom of Heaven
	Circular action that starts in the self, continues to others, and starts over	Blessings to the world

The combination of the Beatitudes and the elements that lead to salvation is very interesting and powerful to me because they intertwine and support each other. For instance, coming to terms with the need for a savior makes you humble, and the Beatitudes that refer to poverty of spirit, gentleness, and mercy require humility. What's more, the Beatitudes show the progression of a person moving toward God, as do the elements leading to salvation.

You may be wondering why I have not included any discussion of Matt. 5:11–12. These verses seem to be a continuation and more personal application of verse 10. Verse 10 refers to "those who have been persecuted," while verse 11 speaks to "you"; verse 10 refers to persecution because of righteousness, while verse 11 speaks of persecution because of "me." I chose not to pursue any more detailed elaboration than I did in Chapter Eight since righteousness is in Jesus, and Jesus is righteousness.

There is good news and better news: the short-term result of hearing, believing, and acting upon that belief can be persecution, but the long-term result is the Kingdom of Heaven!

Notice that becoming poor in spirit and being persecuted both result in the Kingdom of Heaven being ours. Salvation depends on our admitting we are spiritually poverty-stricken and in need of help outside of ourselves. When we submit to Jesus and do his will, we are given the Kingdom.

What is your faith condition? Do you need to repent? Do you need to contact a Bible-believing church to make your confession of Christ and to be baptized? I urge you to do it now.

Chapter Nine's Bible references:

Rom. 10:17
So faith comes by hearing, and hearing by the word of God.

Acts 16:29–31
He called for lights and sprang in, and, fell down trembling before Paul and Silas, and brought them out and said, "Sirs, what must I do to be saved?" They said, "Believe in the Lord Jesus Christ, and you will be saved, you and your household."

Acts 2:38
Peter said to them, "Repent and be baptized, every one of you, in the name of Jesus Christ for the forgiveness of sins, and you will receive the gift of the Holy Spirit."

Rom. 10:9–10
. . . that if you will confess with your mouth that Jesus is Lord, and believe in your heart that God raised him from the dead, you will be saved. For with the heart, one believes unto righteousness; and with the mouth confession is made unto salvation.

Rom. 6:3–5
Or don't you know that all we who were baptized into Christ Jesus were baptized into his death? We were buried therefore with him through baptism to death, that just like Christ was raised from the dead through the glory of the Father, so we also might walk in newness of life. For if we have become united with him in the likeness of his death, we will also be part of his resurrection.

James 2:14–17
What good is it, my brothers, if a man says he has faith, but has no works? Can faith save him? And if a brother or sister is naked and in lack of daily food, and one of you tells them, "Go in peace, be warmed and filled;" and yet you didn't give them the things the body needs, what good is it? Even so faith, if it has no works, is dead in itself.

Matt. 28:18–20
Jesus came to them and spoke to them, saying, "All authority has been given to me in heaven and on earth. Go, and make disciples of all nations, baptizing them in the name of the Father and of the Son and of the Holy Spirit, teaching them to observe all things that I commanded you. Behold, I am with you always, even to the end of the age." Amen.

Matt. 5:11–12
Blessed are you when people reproach you, persecute you, and say all kinds of evil against you falsely, for my sake. Rejoice, and be exceedingly glad, for great is your reward in heaven. For that is how they persecuted the prophets who were before you.

Chapter Ten

Two Journeys or One?

Are we looking at one set of standards and blessings in the Beatitudes and another in the elements leading to salvation? I believe the two interlace and that we must study and act upon both to reach our full potential as God's people.

Studying and acting upon the truths of the Beatitudes can lead to a fuller, closer walk with the Lord. To obediently enter into the Christian adventure, a person must believe and act upon the truths of the Gospel. Then our journey continues with the Beatitudes to guide and inspire us. It is as fruitless to try to incorporate the conditions, attitudes, and actions of the Beatitudes into our lives without coming to him in faith, repentance and baptism as it is to try to live a life in him without using the Beatitudes as our guide. We are on one journey, drawing ever closer to God, the Creator of the entire universe.

I believe most people who hear about the blessings and rewards of the Beatitudes will want them for themselves. To reach these goals, must they progress through hearing, believing, repenting, confessing, being baptized, and living for Christ as his slave and his brother? Jesus answered, "I am the way, the truth, and the life. No one comes to the Father except through me" (John 14:6). The rewards are promised to people who apply the attitudes and actions of the Beatitudes to their lives.

It appears that the first four Beatitudes are meant to connect us with the flow of the life of God and that, in the last four, God is turning to us and saying, "This is my person." The poor in spirit receive the Kingdom of Heaven, the mournful have someone standing with them, the gentle inherit the land that was promised, and the hungry are satiated. Then the merciful receive mercy, the pure in heart see God, the dispensers of peace are called children of God, and the persecuted have the Kingdom. To have mercy, to see God, the Creator, to be called his child, and to own the kingdom—what could be better or more wonderful than these blessings? I say, "Nothing at all."

This life in him is not a destination; it is a journey toward the Lord, an adventure in faith. We will never fully reach the perfection we are pointed toward in the Beatitudes as long as we exist in the imperfect tents that are our human bodies. But, with God's Holy Spirit in us helping along the way, we can strive toward the ideals of being poor in spirit, mourning, being gentle, hungering and thirsting for righteousness, being merciful, being pure in heart, being peacemakers, and enduring persecution for our Christ-like way of life. These are qualities in which we should continually grow and to which we should always aspire.

What amazing blessings we Christians have from the God and Father of our Lord Jesus Christ! He has given us every spiritual blessing; there is no spiritual blessing we could think of that he has not given us. Paul was inspired to write about this in Ephesians 1:1-3:

> Paul, an apostle of Christ Jesus through the will of God, to the saints who are at Ephesus, and the faithful in Christ Jesus: Grace to you and peace from God our Father and the Lord Jesus Christ. Blessed be the God and Father of our Lord Jesus Christ, who has blessed us with every spiritual blessing in the heavenly places in Christ.

If you are in Jesus, I hope this study has helped you along your walk with him. If you are not, I pray that you come to Jesus in faith to begin the journey of life in him. It is truly a blessed adventure!